SCIENCE

CAN BE FUN

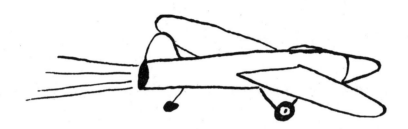

By

Munro Leaf

J. B. LIPPINCOTT COMPANY

PHILADELPHIA AND NEW YORK

SCIENCE IS REALLY KNOWING THE TRUTH

ABOUT THE WORLD WE LIVE IN.

We can't find out the truth about anything by just sitting around and GUESSING—

that's lazy!

And we can't find out the truth by just silly WISHING or HOPING—

that's crazy!

But we can find things out by looking and listening and thinking about what we see and hear. In that way we learn more and more each day and begin to understand the world around us.

SCIENCE CAN BE FUN

and this book is going to help you to find out the

TRUTH

about some of your world.

First, let's think about DAY and NIGHT.

Why is there
DAY LIGHT
part of the time

DARK NIGHT
part of the time?

and

Well, the EARTH that we live on is

a big, round ball moving in space.

The SUN is another big, round, burning ball in space. It shines on the earth.

SO,

let's see what happens when light shines on a ball.

Take a ball into a dark room or closet and shine a flashlight on it. You will see that the light shines on one side of the ball while the other side is dark.

Our big ball called EARTH is spinning around like a top.

And while it is turning round and round it is also moving around the SUN. If you want to find out how our ball of EARTH moves so that we have DAY LIGHT part of the time and DARK NIGHT part of the time,

DO THIS:

Get an orange and push a pencil right through the middle of it so you can hold on to the pencil ends and turn it round and round

LIKE
THIS

(A ball of clay will do just as well, but it won't taste so good when you have finished.)

Now have a grownup get a lighted candle and put it on a table in the middle of a dark room.

Pretend that the candle is the SUN that is sending out light and heat. The SUN looks little to us because it is so far away. It is really a million times bigger than our EARTH.

OUR
EARTH

SUN

Now spin the orange around and pretend it is our EARTH. You will see that the side nearest to the candle is in the light and the side farthest from the candle is in the dark.

Now make a little spot about halfway up the top side of the orange to mark about where you live on our real EARTH.

LIKE
THIS

When you spin the orange you will see that the mark where you live is in the light part of the time and in the dark the rest of the time. When your part of the  Earth is turned away from the Sun and it is dark, you are usually in bed and sound asleep.

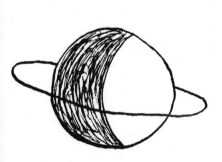

But while you are sleeping our old EARTH keeps on turning, so when you wake up in the morning you are on the sunny side again and there is daylight.

Keep your orange and candle ready and we will see if we can show why, in most parts of the world, part of the year is cold and part hot — Winter and Summer.

This is harder, but it is very interesting.

While our ball of EARTH is spinning from day to night it is also moving around the SUN—

just the way

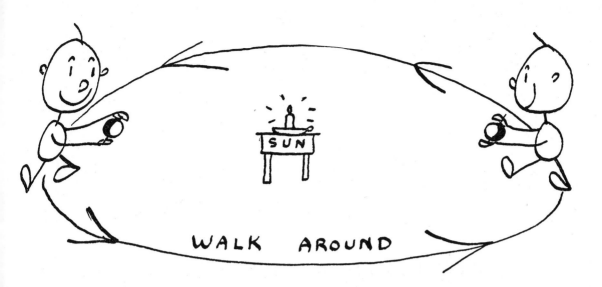

WALK AROUND

you can walk around the candle in the middle of your room while you spin the orange from day to night.

Our EARTH really takes about 365 day and night spins or one whole year while it is moving around the SUN back to where it started from. The reason that it is colder where you live in the Winter than it is in the Summer is just this:

OUR EARTH
ISN'T SPINNING
STRAIGHT UP
LIKE THIS

IT IS ALWAYS
LEANING OVER
A LITTLE BIT
LIKE THIS.

So on its year-long trip around the SUN

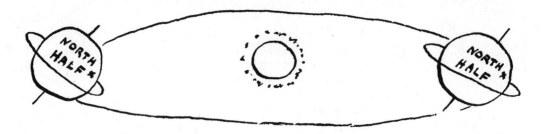

the northern half of the earth, where we live, is tipped part of the time toward the SUN, so we get more sunlight and our days are longer and hotter in Summer.

When our northern half is tipped away from the SUN our days are shorter and we have the cold of Wintertime.

If our EARTH didn't get light and heat from the SUN for part of every day, nothing could grow or stay alive on it.

There is another big ball out in space that is called the MOON.

It moves around the EARTH while the EARTH moves around the SUN.

MOON GOES AROUND US AND WE BOTH GO AROUND SUN

It takes nearly a month to go around our earth. Like the earth, the moon is lighted on only one side at a time by the sun.
From where we are on earth we sometimes can see only a bit of that lighted half — like this:

And other times we can see the whole half lighted like this:

We call that a full moon.

We can't go sit on the Moon and look back at our Earth.

BUT

we can go outdoors and look at the **LIVING THINGS** around us.

We know we are alive. What else can we see that is ALIVE?

Well, we can see other people

and animals of all sorts.

DOGS CATS HORSES COWS SHEEP PIGS SQUIRRELS RABBITS

Did you know that birds are animals too?

				CRABS
SNAKES	FROGS	TURTLES	FISH	LOBSTERS
				CLAMS

FLIES BEES FLEAS BUTTERFLIES AND
GRASSHOPPERS.

In science they are
all called ANIMAL
LIFE, from Elephants
to Tiny Germs.

How many kinds of Animal Life have
you seen?

There are other things alive on our Earth besides people and Animal Life. Do you know what we call them?

PLANT LIFE

That means

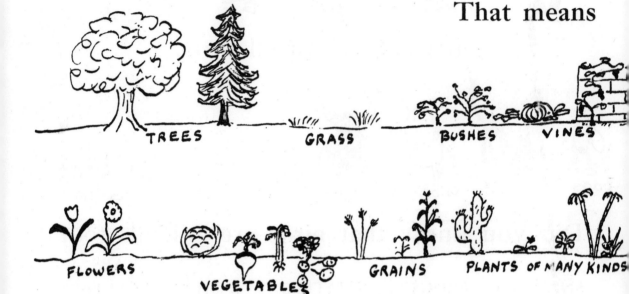

TREES   GRASS   BUSHES   VINES

FLOWERS   VEGETABLES   GRAINS   PLANTS OF MANY KINDS

We call them all Plant Life.

How many kinds of Plant Life can you see right now?

You know that YOU have to have food and water to keep on living.

BUT

do you know that all

ANIMAL LIFE   and   PLANT LIFE

have to have food and water too?

If they get food and water then they can grow big enough and old enough to start new animals or plants that will live and grow too.

Cats have kittens and trees start little trees.

Let's think about
how they get that
FOOD and WATER.

We shall start with Plant Life because Plant Life can do something that

ANIMAL LIFE and PEOPLE

can't do.

Plant Life *can make the food it needs.*

Plants take Water from the ground and Gas from the air, and if the Sun shines on them they can make the food they need to grow.

Do you want to watch some grow?

Remember this takes time and you have to be patient.

Line a glass jar with a piece of paper towel.

Put some radish seeds or grass seeds or lima bean seeds between the paper and the glass. Put them about halfway up the side of the jar so they don't fall in the water.

Keep about an inch of water in the bottom of the jar.

Set the jar by a window where the sun shines on the seeds and leave it there for a while and

BE PATIENT.

After a few days you will see that the seeds have started to grow.

In the Spring get someone to help you plant seeds in the ground or in a box of dirt the way the seed package suggests.

There is enough food in a seed to feed the tiny plant until it is big enough to make food for itself. Each new plant will grow until it has three things:

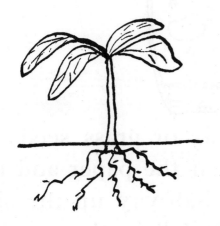

LEAVES

A STEM
OR STALK

ROOTS

When it has these three things it can make its own food.

Through its Roots it takes in WATER that has picked up minerals by dissolving them from the ground. The plant sends the water through its Stem to the Leaves. The Leaves take Gas from the Air, and if the Sun shines on them they mix it with Water to make FOOD. Then the plant stores that food all over itself and grows bigger and bigger.

If you want to see how water travels up the stem of a plant, put a stalk of celery in a glass with about an inch of water in it. Mix ink in the water. After a while the inky water moves up the stalk to the leaves.

You can color white flowers this way if you put Easter egg dyes in water. When the plant is old and big enough it makes seeds that will start new plants like itself. In that way our Earth has new Plant Life all the time.

It is a good thing for us and the Animal Life that this is true because We can't make Food out of Air and Water.

SO

We people and the Animals get our food from Plant Life or from Animals that eat Plant Life.

People eat Chickens that eat insects that eat plants.

Cats eat Fish that eat other fish that eat plant life in the sea.

We and animals eat different parts of plants.

Think of the leaves that are eaten by us

CABBAGE SPINACH LETTUCE SPROUTS KALE MINT

and think of the grass leaves and tree and bush and plant leaves that animals eat.

Then think of the stems, like celery and asparagus, and the sugar from the stalks of sugar cane and the maple syrup that comes out of the trunks of maple trees.

We are eating roots when we eat beets, carrots, turnips, radishes and sweet potatoes

AND

we and the animals love to eat seeds or the
fruit that grows to hold the seeds.

Nuts are seeds and grains of corn or
wheat, oats, rice — they are all seeds.

Even spaghetti and bread and pie crust
are made from ground-up seeds.

Think of the fruit we like that holds the
seeds:

APPLES PEACHES PEARS PLUMS CHERRIES GRAPEFRUIT
and Lemons from trees. Did you know
tomatoes are fruit?

Strawberries — blackberries — blueberries from bushes,
and grapes and raisins from vines.

We even eat flowers like cauliflower and broccoli.

Yes, we eat plant life all right.

Another thing we eat is the food that a hen stores in
an egg to feed the baby chick until it is big enough to
find food for itself. And we drink milk that a cow uses
to feed a baby calf until it can get grass for itself.

BUT

Hens and Cows have to eat plant life to get that food.

Plant Life People and Animal Life
all need WATER.

Let's find out some things about it.

Water doesn't always look the same.

When it runs out of a spigot or a hose and
we can pour and drink it or take a bath and
swim in it, or sail a boat on it — then we
call it a

LIQUID.

But when water gets cold enough to freeze and becomes hard so it has a shape then we say that water is a SOLID.

Ice is a water solid. You can pick it up and break it.

You can slide on it or skate on it.
Snow is a water solid too.

If you look carefully at snowflakes, you will see different shapes, but they all have six sides or rays.

When water gets hot enough it does something else. It becomes a gas that we call Steam or Water Vapor. We can't even see it while it floats in the air. But when it cools enough to change back to liquid drops we can see them, even though they are little and light enough to float in the air.

Clouds and Fogs and Mist are all made from Water Vapor that has cooled enough to become tiny liquid drops that we can see. Heat from the Sun or heat from a stove can make the water change its shape from Solid to Liquid to Gas or Vapor.

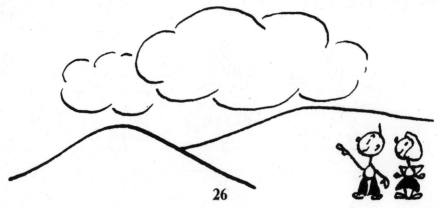

	ON THE STOVE	ON OUR EARTH
S O L I D	Have somebody help you put a piece of solid ice in a pan on a hot stove. As it gets warmer you will see it melt and become a liquid.	In Winter, when it is cold enough, some of the water in lakes and ponds and rivers is solid ice. Snow is frozen water from clouds and it stays on the ground for days until the heat from the Sun melts it.
L I Q U I D	When your piece of ice has melted you can pour it or drink it and a plant could take it through its roots.	When water will pour, then it can move over our Earth. It goes into the ground and runs from streams to rivers and lakes or to the oceans that cover a lot of our ball of Earth.
G A S O R V A P O R	As the water gets hotter, more and more goes into the air until it has all left the pan. You won't see it until it cools to become liquid again and floats in little puffs or clouds.	The hot sunshine makes some of the water in oceans and lakes and rivers go into the air. There, when it cools and becomes liquid drops again, we can see it as big puffs that we call clouds.
	Hold a cold lid over your pan and watch the cooled vapor become liquid again and come drip-dropping down.	When the water in clouds cools enough to stick together in big drops—down comes the water that we call RAIN.

Here is something else that water does. Water can pick up things from the ground and carry them along into the roots of plants.

Put some salt in a glass and stir it for a while. You won't see the salt, but the water will be salty. We say the salt dissolved in the water.

The water in the ocean tastes salty because the rain that went from the ground to the ocean picked up salt on the way.

Put a saucer with a little water in it on a hot radiator or in the sunshine for a few hours and go back to look at it.

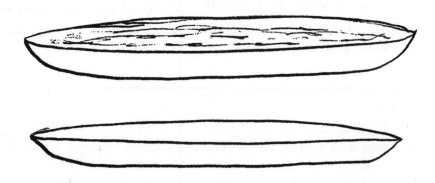

Where did it go?

So far in SCIENCE we have thought mostly about things we can see around us, like:

PEOPLE   ANIMAL LIFE   PLANT LIFE   FOOD   WATER

We can also see the rocks our Earth is made of and the soil on top of the rocks. Soil is a mixture of ground-up tiny pieces of rock and old dead plants and animals.

Now

let's think about some of the things

WE CAN'T SEE.

We know they are there, because we can watch what they do to things that we can see.

We call this part of the book

PUSH and PULL

because these things around us we can't see are pushing and pulling and moving all the time.

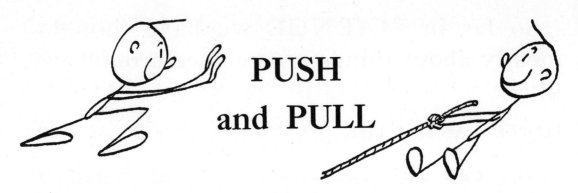

PUSH
and PULL

The biggest PUSHER that is moving around us all the time is

AIR.

We can't see *it,* but we can see things being moved by it — like dust or the leaves and branches on trees and flags flying, or clothes flapping on a clothesline.

When it pushes hard in one direction we can even feel it pushing against us.

What is this stuff called

AIR

?

Air is a mixture of gasses, and even though we can't see those gasses, we know they are there. Everything in the world is either a solid or a liquid or a gas. By doing different things to them like heating or cooling or putting them under pressure, we can change most matter from one form to the other.

GASSES weigh something, and they take up space. A football full of air weighs more than an empty one.

Watch AIR take up space.

If you turn a glass full of air upside down and push it down into a wash basin of water — you will see how the air takes up space and pushes the water so it can't fill the glass.

Turn the glass over and let the air out. Then the glass will fill all the way up with water — and sink.

When you are indoors the air is pushing on you about as much from one direction as another, so you don't feel its pushing.

But watch this. (Do this where it won't matter if you spill.)

Take a glass filled to the tip top with water and put a thin piece of cardboard over it — like this:

Turn it upside down quickly and then take your hand away from the cardboard.

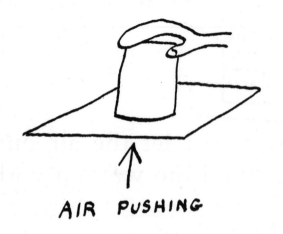

The air pushing up against the cardboard will keep the water in the glass.

When AIR becomes cold it gets heavier and sinks down toward the Earth.

You can see that cold air doesn't take up as much space as hot air.

Put a milk bottle full of air upside down in a bowl of water and mark how high the water comes up inside the bottle.

Put them in the refrigerator for an hour or two.

When you go back you will see that the cold air takes up less space now and has let more water go up higher into the bottle.

When AIR gets hot it pushes and takes up more space. It is lighter than cold air, so it moves up and away from the heavier cold air that is near the ground.

We say that HOT AIR RISES.

Blow some soap bubbles near a fire in a fireplace, or over a hot radiator and watch the hot air push them up and up.

A light feather or tiny piece of tissue paper will be pushed up, too.

Watch where the smoke from a candle or a pipe goes when it is pushed by hot or cold air in a room.

As the AIR around our Earth gets hotter or colder it rises and sinks and moves and pushes. AIR moving fast around our Earth is what we call the

WIND.

Even though you can't see the air that is moving, you can see things being pushed by it, so you know it is there and is real.

Watch the wind push a sailboat.

You can make a toy sailboat move across a tub by blowing air against it yourself.

With so much air pushing around us you might think we would all get pushed off our Earth and blown into space.

BUT WE DON'T.

Even the Air itself can't get too far away from Earth

BECAUSE

coming from the center of our ball of earth, that is bigger than we are, there is a strong, strong

PULL

on us that we call

GRAVITY

You can't see *it,* but you can easily find out what it does.

Jump up into the air.

You have left our Earth **BUT** what happens?

GRAVITY
PULLS YOU

and down you come
— back to Earth

Throw something away from Earth — a stick or stone or ball or piece of paper. Back it will come again, sooner or later, because GRAVITY pulls it.

Birds and insects can fly away from Earth for a while, but when they stop working their wings they come down again, too.

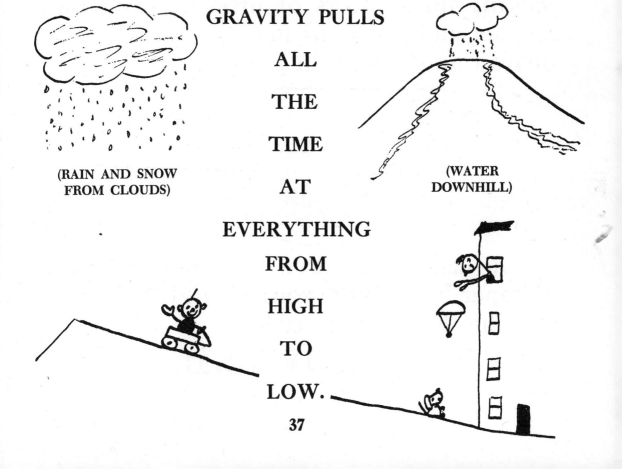

GRAVITY PULLS

ALL

THE

TIME

AT

EVERYTHING

FROM

HIGH

TO

LOW.

(RAIN AND SNOW
FROM CLOUDS)

(WATER
DOWNHILL)

We speak of a PUSH or PULL as a
FORCE.
So we call the pulling that gravity does
the FORCE OF GRAVITY.

If you will get a toy MAGNET from a store, you can watch another FORCE working.

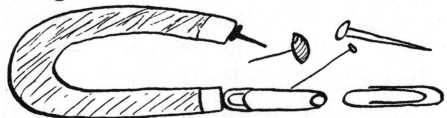

Magnets pull certain things to them. Try picking up all sorts of little things with a magnet and you will find that things made of iron and steel will jump to it.

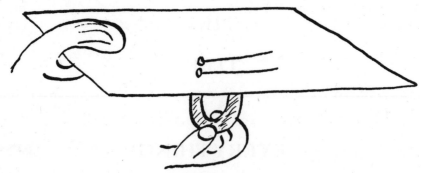

You can even move pins across a piece of paper by pulling your MAGNET under it. This FORCE is called
MAGNETISM.

Do you know that there is a place way up near the North Pole that pulls magnetized needles so that they will point toward it?

Get somebody to show you a COMPASS.

You will see that, no matter how you turn it, the needle always points the same way — toward that place up North on Earth called the Magnetic Pole.

If you rub a sewing needle with one end of your toy magnet about twenty times (always stroking toward the point) you can put it on a cork in a saucer of water and watch it swing around to point North.

You can make your own compass.

Now for the littlest bits of anything in our whole world. They are even smaller than the specks of gas we can't see But everything is made of them.

They are called

ELECTRONS and PROTONS

and when we talk about their pushing and pulling of each other, we call it

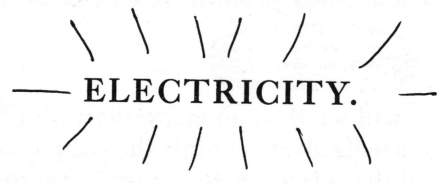

— ELECTRICITY. —

Do you want to take some out of your own hair? All you need to do it with is a comb and a little piece of paper.

Run your comb through your hair about twenty times and put it close to the piece of paper. You will see the paper jump to the comb because

Electricity is working.

The force of Electricity that makes the paper move to the comb is just a weak, little one, but SCIENCE has taught people how to make ELECTRONS and PROTONS move and work for us in powerful and wonderful ways —

We can light our houses with Electricity and make HEAT with it when we are cold

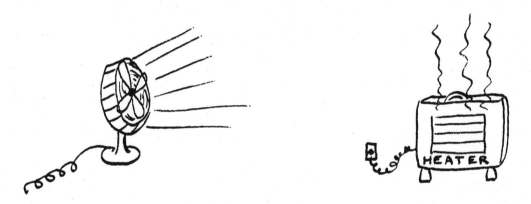

or make it cool us when we are hot. We can send sounds and pictures around the world by using the force of Electricity. Telephones, Radio and Television are all run by it.

If we watch carefully we can see people using Forces in ways we hadn't thought about before.

Look at a seesaw work.

(Gravity is pulling both ends, but the two people balance and both stay up a while.)

See how one person can hold up several people if his end of the board is longer than theirs —

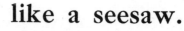

Now you see why a man can move a heavy weight if he uses a LEVER that is like a seesaw.

That is using SCIENCE.

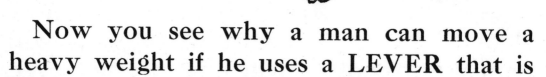

Do you know that it is easier to shovel snow or sweep dirt with long handles on our shovels and brooms instead of short ones? Try both and find out WHY?

Long ago there was a man who had to get a heavy stone to the top of a high place.

You know how much easier his work would have been if he had known that he could pull it up a slope, or better yet that he could

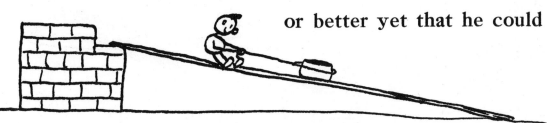

put rollers under it, or still better yet that he could make a cart on wheels to carry the stone,

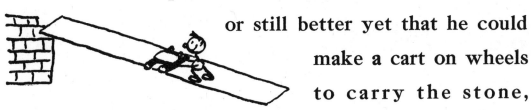

and teach an animal to pull it for him.

But men didn't always know these things. They had to learn.

Now SCIENCE has taught us to make all sorts of machines to make our work easier. Think of the machines like

MOTORCYCLES

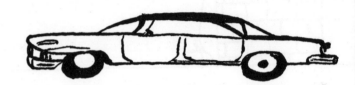

AUTOS

PLANES

TRAINS

and BOATS

that Science has given us today so that we can go from one place to another more quickly and comfortably than by walking or swimming.

All these machines run because

SCIENCE

found ways to make the

PUSH and PULL

of FORCE work for us.

Your automobile runs because a spark of

ELECTRICITY

makes

GAS or VAPOR,

that was a liquid,

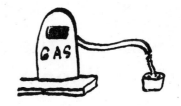

explode and push its way out

of a tight little space in your engine.

Pushing to get out, it turns a rod

that is connected with the wheels.

They turn, and away you go.

The jet planes you see in the sky burn oil that turns into Gas and when it explodes it pushes out from the back of the plane.

When the hot gas goes out the hole in the back — the plane gets pushed to the front.

Blow up a toy balloon.

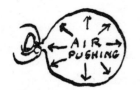

Hold the air in. Then let it go. You will see that while the air rushed out of the hole — the balloon was pushed the other way.

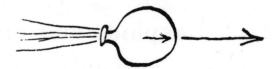

That is why jets and rockets fly.

Men are making rockets now that push out into space and go circling around our Earth like little moons.

Almost every day some man or woman who was once a boy or girl like you, finds out something new about our world.

Only a few years ago some SCIENTISTS found out that by putting certain things from our Earth together, they could make more power than we ever had used before.

So now we have submarines
that can go around the world
with the PUSH they get
from something no bigger
than a baseball.

We call this force

ATOMIC POWER.

Looking, Listening and Thinking carefully
may help you to find some new
truths that will make living
on this ball of
EARTH

MORE FUN
FOR
EVERYBODY.

LET'S TRY IT.

1339